Art and Lecture Outlines

for

Weiten's

Psychology

Art and Lecture Outlines

for

Weiten's

Psychology
Themes and Variations
Seventh Edition

Brian Malley
University of Michigan

THOMSON

WADSWORTH

Australia • Brazil • Canada • Mexico • Singapore • Spain • United Kingdom • United States

Printer: Thomson West

ISBN 0-495-17047-X

Thomson Higher Education
10 Davis Drive
Belmont, CA 94002-3098
USA

For more information about our products, contact us at:
Thomson Learning Academic Resource Center
1-800-423-0563

For permission to use material from this text or product, submit a request online at
http://www.thomsonrights.com.
Any additional questions about permissions can be submitted by email to
thomsonrights@thomson.com.

Table of Contents

Chapter 1: The Evolution of Psychology

**From Speculation to Science:
How Psychology Developed**

- Prior to 1879
  - Physiology and philosophy scholars studying questions about the mind

- Wilhelm Wundt (1832-1920) University of Leipzig, Germany
  - Campaigned to make psychology an independent discipline
  - Established the first laboratory for the study of psychology in 1879

- Psychology was born

Wilhelm Wundt's International Influence

- Leipzig, the place to study psychology
  - Graduates of Wundt's program set up new labs across Europe and North America

- G. Stanley Hall (1846-1924), Johns Hopkins University
  - Established the first psychology laboratory in the U.S. in 1883

- Between 1883 and 1893, 24 new laboratories in North America

The Battle of the "Schools" in the U.S.: Structuralism vs. Functionalism

- Structuralism – Edward Titchener
  - Analyze consciousness into basic elements
  - Introspection – careful, systematic observations of one's own conscious experience

- Functionalism – William James
  - Investigate function of consciousness
  - Led to investigation of mental testing, developmental patterns, and sex differences

Sigmund Freud and the Concept of the Unconscious Mind

- Sigmund Freud (1856-1939): Austria

- Founded Psychoanalytic school of thought

- Emphasis on unconscious processes influencing behavior
  - Unconscious = outside awareness

Freud's Ideas: Controversy and Influence

- Behavior is influenced by the unconscious
- Unconscious conflict related to sexuality plays a central role in behavior
- Controversial notions caused debate/resistance
- Significant influence on the field of psychology

Behaviorism: Redefining Psychology

- John B. Watson (1878-1958): United States
  - Founder of Behaviorism
- Psychology = scientific study of behavior
- Behavior = overt or observable responses or activities
  - Radical reorientation of psychology as a science of observable behavior
  - Study of consciousness abandoned

John Watson and the Nature-Nurture Debate

- Nurture, not nature
  - "give me a dozen healthy infants, well-formed, and my own special world to bring them up in and I'll guarantee to take any one at random and train him to become any type of specialist I might select – doctor, lawyer, artist, merchant-chief, and yes, even beggar-man and thief…"
- Behaviorist school of thought emphasized the environment (nurture)
- Focus on stimulus-response relationships
- S-R psychology

Are People Free?
B.F. Skinner

- B.F. Skinner (1904-1990): United States
  - Environmental factors determine behavior
  - Responses that lead to positive outcomes are repeated
  - Responses that lead to negative outcomes are not repeated
  - *Beyond Freedom and Dignity*
  - More controversy regarding free will

The 1950's: Opposition to Psychoanalytic Theory and Behaviorism
- Charges that both were de-humanizing
- Diverse opposition groups got together to form a loose alliance
- A new school of thought emerged - Humanism
    - Led by Abraham Maslow (1908-1970) and Carl Rogers (1902-1987)
    - Emphasis on the unique qualities of humans: freedom and personal growth

Putting the Psyche Back in Psychology:
The Return of Cognition

- Cognition = mental processes involved in acquiring knowledge

- 1950's and 60's – Piaget, Chomsky, and Simon
    - Application of scientific methods to studying internal mental events
    - **Cognitive psychology: the new dominant perspective?**

Biological Psychology:
The Biological Basis of Behavior

- Biological perspective - behavior explained in terms of physiological processes
    - James Olds (1956)
        - Electrical stimulation of the brain evokes emotional responses in animals
    - Roger Sperry (1981)
        - Left and right brain specialization

Cultural Psychology:
Recognizing Human Variation

- Ethnocentrism – viewing one's own group as superior and as the standard for judging

- Historically: middle and upper class white males studying middle and upper class white males

- 1980's – increased interest in how cultural factors influence behavior

- Growing global interdependence

- Increased cultural diversity

Evolutionary Psychology:
Human Adaptations

- Central premise: natural selection occurs for behavioral, as well as physical, characteristics

- Buss, Daly & Wilson, Cosmides & Tooby – 80's and 90's
  - Studied natural selection of mating preferences, jealousy, aggression, sexual behavior, language, decision making, personality, and development

- Thought provoking perspective gaining in influence, but not without criticism

Positive Psychology

- Martin Seligman's epiphany
- Humanist concerns revisited
- Uses theory and research to better understand the positive, creative, and fulfilling aspects of human existence
  - Positive subjective experiences
  - Positive individual traits
  - Positive institutions and communities

Psychology Today:
A Thriving Science and Profession

- Psychology is the science that studies behavior and the physiological and cognitive processes that underlie it, and it is the profession that applies the accumulated knowledge of this science to practical problems.

- Research: Seven major areas
- Applied Psychology: Four major areas

Studying Psychology:
Seven Organizing Themes

- Psychology as a field of study:
  - Empirical
  - Theoretically diverse
  - Evolves in sociohistorical context

- Behavior:
  - Determined by multiple causes
  - Shaped by cultural heritage
  - Influenced jointly by heredity and environment

- People's experience of the world is highly subjective.

Chapter 2: The Research Enterprise in Psychology

The Scientific Approach:
A Search for Laws

- Basic assumption: events are governed by some lawful order

- Goals:
  - Measurement and description
  - Understanding and prediction
  - Application and control

The Scientific Method: Terminology

- **Operational definitions** are used to clarify precisely what is meant by each variable

- **Participants** or **subjects** are the organisms whose behavior is systematically observed in a study

- **Data collection techniques** allow for empirical observation and measurement

- **Statistics** are used to analyze data and decide whether hypotheses were supported

The Scientific Method: Terminology

- Findings are shared through reports at **scientific meetings** and in **scientific journals** – periodicals that publish echnical and scholarly material
  - Advantages of the scientific method: clarity of communication and relative intolerance of error

- **Research methods**: general strategies for conducting scientific studies

Experimental Research:
Looking for Causes

- **Experiment** = manipulation of one variable under controlled conditions so that resulting changes in another variable can be observed
  - Detection of cause-and-effect relationships

- Independent variable (IV) = variable manipulated

- Dependent variable (DV) = variable affected by manipulation
  - How does X affect Y?
  - X = Independent Variable, and Y = Dependent Variable

Experimental and Control Groups: The Logic of the Scientific Method

- Experimental group
- Control group
  - Random assignment
  - Manipulate independent variable for one group only
  - Resulting differences in the two groups must be due to the independent variable
- Extraneous and confounding variables

Experimental Designs: Variations

- Expose a single group to two different conditions
  - Reduces extraneous variables
- Manipulate more than one independent variable
  - Allows for study of interactions between variables
- Use more than one dependent variable
  - Obtains a more complete picture of effect of   the independent variable

Strengths and Weaknesses of Experimental Research

- Strengths:
  - conclusions about cause-and-effect can be drawn
- Weaknesses:
  - artificial nature of experiments
  - ethical and practical issues

Descriptive/Correlational Methods: Looking for Relationships

- **Methods** used when a researcher cannot manipulate the variables under study
  - **Naturalistic observation**
  - **Case studies**
  - **Surveys**
- Allow researchers to describe patterns of behavior and discover links or associations between variables but cannot imply causation

Statistics and Research: Drawing Conclusions

- **Statistics** – using mathematics to organize, summarize, and interpret numerical data
  - **Descriptive statistics**: organizing and summarizing data
  - **Inferential statistics**: interpreting data and drawing conclusions

Descriptive Statistics:
Measures of Central Tendency

- **Measures of central tendency** = typical or average score in a distribution

- **Mean**: arithmetic average of scores

- **Median**: score falling in the exact center

- **Mode**: most frequently occurring score
  - Which most accurately depicts the typical?

Descriptive Statistics:
Variability

- **Variability** = how much scores vary from each other and from the mean
  - **Standard deviation** = numerical depiction of variability

- High variability in data set = high standard deviation

- Low variability in data set = low standard deviation

Descriptive Statistics: Correlation

- When two variables are related to each other, they are **correlated**.

- **Correlation** = numerical index of degree of relationship
  - Correlation expressed as a number **between 0 and 1**
  - Can be **positive or negative**
  - Numbers closer to 1 (+ or -) indicate stronger relationship

Correlation:
Prediction, Not Causation

- Higher correlation coefficients = increased ability to predict one variable based on the other
  - SAT/ACT scores moderately correlated with first year college GPA

- 2 variables may be highly correlated, but not causally related
  - Foot size and vocabulary positively correlated
  - Do larger feet cause larger vocabularies?
  - The third variable problem

Inferential Statistics:
Interpreting Data and Drawing Conclusions

- Hypothesis testing: do observed findings support the hypotheses?
  - Are findings real or due to chance?

- Statistical significance = when the probability that the observed findings are due to chance is very low
  - Very low = less than 5 chances in 100/ .05 level

Evaluating Research:
Methodological Pitfalls

- Sampling bias

- Placebo effects

- Distortions in self-report data:
  - Social desirability bias
  - Response set

- Experimenter bias
  - the **double-blind** solution

Ethics in Psychological Research:
Do the Ends Justify the Means?

- The question of **deception**

- The question of **animal research**
  - Controversy among psychologists and the public

- Ethical standards for research: the **American Psychological Association**
  - Ensures both human and animal subjects are treated with dignity

Chapter 3: The Biological Bases of Behavior

Communication in the Nervous System

- Hardware:
  - **Glia** – structural support and insulation
  - **Neurons** – communication
  - **Soma** – cell body
  - **Dendrites** – receive
  - **Axon** – transmit away

Neural Communication:
Insulation and Information Transfer

- **Myelin sheath** – speeds up transmission

- **Terminal Button** – end of axon; secretes neurotransmitters

- **Neurotransmitters** – chemical messengers

- **Synapse** – point at which neurons interconnect

The Neural Impulse:
Electrochemical Beginnings

- Hodgkin & Huxley (1952) - giant squid
  - Fluids inside and outside neuron
  - Electrically charged particles (ions)
  - Neuron at rest – negative charge on inside compared to outside
  - -70 millivolts – **resting potential**

The Neural Impulse: The Action Potential

- Stimulation causes cell membrane to open briefly

- Positively charged sodium ions flow in

- Shift in electrical charge travels along neuron

- **The Action Potential**

- **Al –or–none law**

The Synapse: Chemicals as Signal Couriers

- Synaptic cleft

- Presynaptic neuron
  - Synaptic vesicles
  - Neurotransmitters

- Postsynaptic neuron
  - Receptor sites

When a Neurotransmitter Binds:
The Postsynaptic Potential

- Voltage change at receptor site – **postsynaptic potential (PSP)**
  - Not all-or-none
  - Changes the probability of the postsynaptic neuron firing

- Positive voltage shift – **excitatory PSP**

- Negative voltage shift – **inhibitory PSP**

Signals: From Postsynaptic Potentials
to Neural Networks

- One neuron, signals from thousands of other neurons

- Requires integration of signals
  - PSPs add up, balance out
  - Balance between IPSPs and EPSPs

- Neural networks
  - Patterns of neural activity
  - Interconnected neurons that fire together or sequentially

Signals: From Postsynaptic Potentials
to Neural Networks

- Synaptic connections
  - Elimination and creation
  - Synaptic pruning

Neurotransmitters

- Specific neurotransmitters work at specific synapses
  - Lock and key mechanism

- **Agonist** – mimics neurotransmitter action

- **Antagonist** – opposes action of a neurotransmitter

- 15 – 20 neurotransmitters known at present

- Interactions between neurotransmitter circuits

Organization of the Nervous System

- Central nervous system (CNS)
  - **Afferent** = toward the CNS
  - **Efferent** = away from the CNS

- Peripheral nervous system
  - Somatic nervous system
  - Autonomic nervous system (ANS)

- Sympathetic

- Parasympathetic

Studying the Brain: Research Methods

- Electroencephalography (EEG)

- Damage studies/lesioning

- Electrical stimulation (ESB)

- Transcranial magnetic stimulation (TMS)

- Brain imaging –
  - computerized tomography
  - positron emission tomography
  - magnetic resonance imaging

Brain Regions and Functions

- **Hindbrain** – vital functions – medulla, pons, and cerebellum

- **Midbrain** – sensory functions – dopaminergic projections, reticular activating system

- **Forebrain** – emotion, complex thought – thalamus, hypothalamus, limbic system, cerebrum, cerebral cortex

The Cerebrum:
Two Hemispheres, Four Lobes

- **Cerebral Hemispheres** – two specialized halves connected by the **corpus collosum**
  - **Left hemisphere** – verbal processing: language, speech, reading, writing
  - **Right hemisphere** – nonverbal processing: spatial, musical, visual recognition

The Cerebrum:
Two Hemispheres, Four Lobes

- Four Lobes:
  - **Occipital** – vision
  - **Parietal** - somatosensory
  - **Temporal** - auditory
  - **Frontal** – movement, executive control systems

The Endocrine System:
Glands and Hormones

- **Hormones** – chemical messengers in the bloodstream
  - Pulsatile release by endocrine glands
  - Negative feedback system

- Endocrine glands
  - **Pituitary** – "master gland," growth hormone
  - **Thyroid** – metabolic rate
  - **Adrenal** – salt and carbohydrate metabolism
  - **Pancreas** – sugar metabolism
  - **Gonads** – sex hormones

Genes and Behavior:
The Field of Behavioral Genetics

- **Behavioral genetics** = the study of the influence of genetic factors on behavioral traits

- **Chromosomes** – strands of **DNA** carrying genetic information
    - Human cells contain **46 chromosomes** in pairs (sex-cells – 23 single)
    - Each chromosome – thousands of genes, also in pairs

- Dominant, recessive

- Homozygous, heterozygous

- Genotype/Phenotype and Polygenic Inheritance

Research Methods in Behavioral Genetics

- **Family studies** – does it run in the family?

- **Twin studies** – compare resemblance of identical (monozygotic) and fraternal (dizygotic) twins on a **trait**

- **Adoption** studies – examine resemblance between adopted children and their biological and adoptive parents

Modern Approaches to the
Nature vs. Nurture Debate

- **Molecular Genetics** = the study of the biochemical bases of genetic inheritance
    - Genetic mapping – locating specific genes - The Human Genome Project

- Behavioral Genetics
    - The interactionist model
    - Richard Rose (1995) – "We inherit dispositions, not destinies."

Evolutionary Psychology:
Behavior in Terms of Adaptive Significance

- Based on Darwin's ideas of **natural selection**
    - Reproductive success key

- **Adaptations** – behavioral as well as physical
    - Fight-or-flight response
    - Taste preferences
    - Parental investment and mating

Chapter 4: Sensation and Perception

Sensation and Perception: The Distinction

- **Sensation**: stimulation of sense organs

- **Perception**: selection, organization, and interpretation of sensory input

- **Psychophysics =** the study of how physical stimuli are translated into psychological experience

Psychophysics: Basic Concepts

- Sensation begins with a detectable stimulus

- **Fechner**: the concept of the threshold
  - **Absolute threshold**: detected 50% of the time
  - **Just noticeable difference (JND)**: smallest difference detectable

- **Weber's law**: size of JND proportional to size of initial stimulus

Psychophysics: Concepts and Issues

- **Signal-Detection Theory**: Sensory processes + decision processes

- **Subliminal Perception**: Existence vs. practical effects

- **Sensory Adaptation**: Decline in sensitivity

Vision: The Stimulus

- **Light** = electromagnetic radiation
  - **Amplitude**: perception of brightness
  - **Wavelength**: perception of color
  - **Purity**: mix of wavelengths
    - Perception of **saturation**, or richness of colors

The Eye:
Converting Light into Neural Impulses

- The eye: housing and channeling

- Components:
  - **Cornea**: where light enters the eye
  - **Lens**: focuses the light rays on the retina
  - **Iris**: colored ring of muscle, constricts or dilates via amount of light
  - **Pupil**: regulates amount of light

The Retina: An Extension of the CNS

- **Retina:** absorbs light, processes images
- **Optic disk:** optic nerve connection/blind spot
- **Receptor cells:**
  - **Rods**: black and white/low light vision
  - **Cones**: color and daylight vision
- **Adaptation:** becoming more or less sensitive to light as needed
- **Information processing:**
  - Receptive fields
  - Lateral antagonism

The Retina and the Brain:
Visual Information Processing

- Light → rods and cones → neural signals → bipolar cells → ganglion cells → optic nerve → optic chiasm → opposite half brain
- Main pathway: lateral geniculate nucleus (thalamus) → primary visual cortex (occipital lobe)
  - magnocellular: where
  - parvocellular: what
- Second pathway: superior colliculus → thalamus → primary visual cortex

Hubel and Wiesel:
Feature Detectors and the Nobel Prize

- Early 1960's: Hubel and Wiesel
  - Microelectrode recording of axons in primary visual cortex of animals
  - Discovered feature detectors: neurons that respond selectively to lines, edges, etc.
  - Groundbreaking research: Nobel Prize in 1981
- Later research: cells specific to faces in the temporal lobes of monkeys and humans

Basics of Color Vision

- **Wavelength** determines color
  - Longer = red / shorter = violet
- **Amplitude** determines brightness
- **Purity** determines saturation

Theories of Color Vision

- **Trichromatic theory** - Young and Helmholtz
  - Receptors for red, green, blue – color mixing

- Opponent Process theory – Hering
  - 3 pairs of antagonistic colors
  - red/green, blue/yellow, black/white

- Current perspective: both theories necessary

Perceiving Forms, Patterns, and Objects

- Reversible figures

- Perceptual sets

- Inattentional blindness

- Feature detection theory - bottom-up processing

- Form perception - top-down processing

- Subjective contours

- Gestalt psychologists: the whole is more than the sum of its parts
  - Reversible figures and perceptual sets demonstrate that the same visual stimulus can result in very different perceptions

Principles of Perception

- Gestalt principles of form perception:
  - figure-ground, proximity, similarity, continuity, closure, and simplicity

- Recent research:
  - **Distal** (stimuli outside the body) vs. **proximal** (stimulus energies impinging on sensory receptors) stimuli
  - **Perceptual hypotheses**

- Context

Depth and Distance Perception

- **Binocular cues** – clues from both eyes together
  - retinal disparity
  - convergence

- **Monocular cues** – clues from a single eye
  - motion parallax
  - accommodation
  - pictorial depth cues

Stability in the Perceptual World:
Perceptual Constancies

- **Perceptual constancies** – stable perceptions amid changing stimuli
  - Size
  - Shape
  - Brightness
  - Hue
  - Location in space

Optical Illusions:
The Power of Misleading Cues

- **Optical Illusions** - discrepancy between visual appearance and physical reality

- Famous optical illusions: **Muller-Lyer Illusion, Ponzo Illusion, Poggendorf Illusion, Upside-Down T Illusion, Zollner Illusion, the Ames Room, and Impossible Figures**

- Cultural differences: Perceptual hypotheses at work

Hearing: The Auditory System

- Stimulus = **sound waves** (vibrations of molecules traveling in air)
  - Amplitude (loudness)
  - Wavelength (pitch)
  - Purity (timbre)

- Wavelength described in terms of **frequency**: measured in **cycles per second (Hz)**
  - Frequency increase = pitch increase

The Ear: Three Divisions

- External ear (pinna): collects sound

- Middle ear: the ossicles (hammer, anvil, stirrup)

- Inner ear: the cochlea
  - a fluid-filled, coiled tunnel
  - contains the **hair cells**, the auditory receptors
  - lined up on the **basilar membrane**

The Auditory Pathway

- Sound waves vibrate bones of the middle ear

- Stirrup hits against the oval window of cochlea

- Sets the fluid inside in motion

- Hair cells are stimulated with the movement of the basilar membrane

- Physical stimulation converted into neural impulses

- Sent through the thalamus to the auditory cortex (temporal lobes)

Theories of Hearing: Place or Frequency?

- Hermann von Helmholtz (1863)
  - Place theory

- Other researchers (Rutherford, 1886)
  - Frequency theory

- Georg von Bekesy (1947)
  - Traveling wave theory

Auditory Localization:
Where Did that Sound Come From?

- Two cues critical:
  - **Intensity** (loudness)
  - **Timing** of sounds arriving at each ear

- Head as "shadow" or partial sound barrier

- Timing differences as small as 1/100,000 of a second

The Chemical Senses: Taste

- Taste (gustation)

- Physical stimulus: soluble chemical substances
  - Receptor cells found in **taste buds**

- Pathway: taste buds -> neural impulse -> thalamus -> cortex
  - Four primary tastes: sweet, sour, bitter, and salty
  - Taste: learned and social processes

The Chemical Senses: Smell

- Smell (Olfaction)

- Physical stimuli: substances carried in the air
  - dissolved in fluid, the mucus in the nose
  - Olfactory receptors = **olfactory cilia**

- Pathway: Olfactory cilia -> neural impulse -> olfactory nerve -> olfactory bulb (brain)
  - Does not go through thalamus

Skin Senses: Touch

- Physical stimuli = mechanical, thermal, and chemical energy impinging on the skin.

- Pathway: **Sensory receptors -> the spinal column -> brainstem -> cross to opposite side of brain -> thalamus -> somatosensory (parietal lobe)**

- **Temperature**: free nerve endings in the skin

- **Pain receptors**: also free nerve endings
  - Two **pain pathways**: fast vs. slow

Other Senses: Kinesthetic and Vestibular

- **Kinesthesis** - knowing the position of the various parts of the body
    - Receptors in joints/muscles

- **Vestibular** - equilibrium/balance
    - Semicircular canals

_____

_____

_____

_____

_____

Chapter 5: Variations in Consciousness

Consciousness: Personal Awareness

- Awareness of Internal and External Stimuli
  - Levels of awareness
- **James** – stream of consciousness
- **Freud** – unconscious
- Sleep/dreaming research

The Electroencephalograph:
A Physiological Index of Consciousness

- **EEG** – monitoring of brain electrical activity
- Brain-waves
  - Amplitude (height)
  - Frequency (cycles per second)
- Beta (13-24 cps)
- Alpha (8-12 cps)
- Theta (4-7 cps)
- Delta (<4 cps)

Biological Rhythms and Sleep

- **Circadian Rhythms** – 24 hr biological cycles
  - Regulation of sleep/other body functions
- Physiological pathway of the biological clock:
  - Light levels → retina → suprachiasmatic nucleus of hypothalamus → pineal gland → secretion of melatonin
- **Melatonin** and circadian rhythms

Sleep/Waking Research

- Instruments:
  - **Electroencephalograph** – brain electrical activity
  - **Electromyograph** – muscle activity
  - **Electrooculograph** – eye movements
  - Other bodily functions also observed

Sleep Stages: Cycling Through Sleep

- **Stage 1**: brief, transitional (1-7 minutes)
  - alpha → theta
  - hypnic jerks

- Stage 2: sleep spindles (10-25 minutes)

- Stages 3 & 4: slow-wave sleep (30 minutes)

- Stage 5: REM, EEG similar to awake, vivid dreaming (first a few minutes, then longer)
  - Developmental differences in REM sleep

The Neural Bases of Sleep

- Brain Structures:
  - Ascending reticular activating system
  - Pons, medulla, thalamus, hypothalamus, limbic system

- Neurotransmitters:
  - Acetylcholine and serotonin
  - Also norepinephrine, dopamine, and GABA

Why Do We Sleep?

- Hypothesis 1:
  - Sleep evolved to conserve organisms' energy

- Hypothesis 2:
  - Immobilization during sleep is adaptive because it reduces danger

- Hypothesis 3:
  - Sleep helps animals to restore energy and other bodily resources

Sleep Deprivation

- Complete deprivation
  - 3 or 4 days max

- Partial deprivation or sleep restriction
  - impaired attention, reaction time, coordination, and decision making
  - accidents: Chernobyl, Exxon Valdez

- Selective deprivation
  - REM and slow-wave sleep: rebound effect

Sleep Problems

- **Insomnia** – difficulty falling or staying asleep
- **Narcolepsy** – falling asleep uncontrollably
- **Sleep Apnea** – reflexive gasping for air that awakens
- **Nightmares** – anxiety arousing dreams - REM
- **Night Terrors** – intense arousal and panic - NREM
- **Somnambulism** – sleepwalking

Dreams and Dreaming:
Content and Significance

- **Dreams** – mental experiences during sleep
  - Content usually familiar
  - Common themes
  - Waking life spillover – day residue
- Western vs. Non-Western interpretations

Hypnosis: Altered State of Consciousness or Role Playing?

- **Hypnosis** = a systematic procedure that increases suggestibility
- **Hypnotic susceptibility**: individual differences
- **Effects produced through hypnosis:**
  - Anesthesia
  - Sensory distortions and hallucinations
  - Disinhibition
  - Posthypnotic suggestions and amnesia

Meditation

- **Meditation** = practices that train attention to heighten awareness and bring mental processes under greater voluntary control
- **Yoga, Zen, transcendental meditation (TM)**
  - Potential physiological benefits
- Similar to effective relaxation procedures

_____
_____
_____
_____
_____
_____
_____
_____
_____
_____
_____
_____
_____
_____
_____
_____
_____
_____
_____
_____
_____
_____
_____
_____

Psychoactive drugs

- Narcotics (opiates) – pain relieving
- Sedatives – sleep inducing
- Stimulants – increase CNS activity
- Hallucinogens – distort sensory and perceptual experience
- Cannabis – produce mild, relaxed euphoria
- Alcohol – produces relaxed euphoria, decreases in inhibitions
- MDMA – produces a warm, friendly euphoria

Chapter 6: Learning

Classical Conditioning

- Ivan Pavlov
- Terminology
  - Unconditioned Stimulus (UCS)
  - Conditioned Stimulus (CS)
  - Unconditioned Response (UCR)
  - Conditioned Response (CR)

Classical Conditioning: More Terminology

- **Trial** = pairing of **UCS** and **CS**
- **Acquisition = initial stage in learning**
- **Stimulus contiguity** = occurring together in time and space

Classical Conditioning: More Terminology

- 3 types of Classical Conditioning
  - **Simultaneous conditioning**: CS and UCS begin and end together
  - **Short-delayed conditioning**: CS begins just before the UCS, end together
  - **Trace conditioning**: CS begins and ends before UCS is presented

Processes in Classical Conditioning

- Extinction
- Spontaneous Recovery
- Stimulus Generalization
- Discrimination
- Higher-order conditioning

**Operant Conditioning
or Instrumental Learning**

- Edward L. Thorndike (1913) – the law of effect
- B.F. Skinner (1953) – principle of reinforcement
  - Operant chamber
  - Emission of response
  - Reinforcement contingencies
  - Cumulative recorder

Basic Processes in Operant Conditioning

- Acquisition
- Shaping
- Extinction
- Stimulus Control
  - Generalization
  - Discrimination

Reinforcement:
Consequences that Strengthen Responses

- Primary Reinforcers
  - Satisfy biological needs
- Secondary Reinforcers
  - Conditioned reinforcement

Schedules of Reinforcement

- Continuous reinforcement
- Intermittent (partial) reinforcement
  - Ratio schedules
- Fixed
- Variable
  - Interval schedules
- Fixed
- Variable

Consequences:
Reinforcement and Punishment

- Increasing a response:
  - **Positive reinforcement** = response followed by rewarding stimulus
  - **Negative reinforcement** = response followed by removal of an aversive stimulus
- Escape learning
- Avoidance learning
- Decreasing a response:
  - Punishment
  - Problems with punishment

**Changes in Our Understanding
of Conditioning**

- Biological Constraints on Conditioning
    - Instinctive Drift
    - Conditioned Taste Aversion
    - Preparedness and Phobias

- Cognitive Influences on Conditioning
    - Signal relations
    - Response-outcome relations

- Evolutionary Perspectives on learning

Observational Learning: Basic Processes

- Albert Bandura (1977, 1986)
    - Observational learning
    - Vicarious conditioning

- 4 key processes
    - attention
    - retention
    - reproduction
    - motivation

- acquisition vs. performance

_____

_____

_____

_____

_____

_____

_____

_____

_____

_____

_____

_____

_____

Chapter 7: Human Memory

Human Memory: Basic Questions

- How does information get **into** memory?

- How is information **maintained** in memory?

- How is information pulled **back out** of memory?

Encoding: Getting Information Into Memory

- The role of **attention**

- Focusing awareness

- **Selective attention** = selection of input
    - **Filtering**: early or late?

Levels of Processing:
Craik and Lockhart (1972)

- Incoming information processed at different levels

- Deeper processing = longer lasting memory codes

- **Encoding levels**:
    - Structural = shallow
    - Phonemic = intermediate
    - Semantic = deep

Enriching Encoding: Improving Memory

- **Elaboration** = linking a stimulus to other information at the time of encoding
    - Thinking of examples

- **Visual Imagery** = creation of visual images to represent words to be remembered
    - Easier for concrete objects: Dual-coding theory

- Self-Referent Encoding
    - Making information personally meaningful

Storage: Maintaining Information in Memory

- Analogy: information storage in computers ~ information storage in human memory

- Information-processing theories
    - Subdivide memory into **3 different stores**

- Sensory, Short-term, Long-term

Sensory Memory

- Brief preservation of information in original sensory form

- Auditory/Visual – approximately ¼ second
    - George Sperling (1960)

- Classic experiment on **visual sensory store**

Short Term Memory (STM)

- Limited capacity – magical number 7 plus or minus 2
  - **Chunking** – grouping familiar stimuli for storage as a single unit

- **Limited duration** – about **20 seconds** without rehearsal
  - **Rehearsal** – the process of repetitively verbalizing or thinking about the information

Short-Term Memory as "Working Memory"

- STM not limited to phonemic encoding

- Loss of information not only due to decay

- **Baddeley (1986)** – 3 components of working memory
  - Phonological rehearsal loop
  - Visuospatial sketchpad
  - Executive control system
  - Long-Term Memory: Unlimited Capacity

- Permanent storage?
  - Flashbulb memories
  - Recall through hypnosis

- Debate: are STM and LTM really different?
  - Phonemic vs. Semantic encoding
  - Decay vs. Interference based forgetting

How is Knowledge Represented and Organized in Memory?

- Clustering and Conceptual Hierarchies

- Schemas and Scripts

- Semantic Networks

- Connectionist Networks and PDP Models

Retrieval: Getting Information Out of Memory

- The tip-of-the-tongue phenomenon – a failure in retrieval
  - Retrieval cues

- Recalling an event
  - Context cues

- Reconstructing memories
  - Misinformation effect

- Source monitoring, reality monitoring

Forgetting: When Memory Lapses

- Retention – the proportion of material retained
  - Recall
  - Recognition
  - Relearning
- Ebbinghaus's Forgetting Curve

Why Do We Forget?

- Ineffective Encoding
- Decay theory
- Interference theory
  - Proactive
  - Retroactive

Retrieval Failure

- Encoding Specificity
- Transfer-Appropriate Processing
- Repression
  - Authenticity of repressed memories?
  - Memory illusions

The Physiology of Memory

- Biochemistry
  - Alteration in synaptic transmission
- Hormones modulating neurotransmitter systems
- Protein synthesis
- **Neural circuitry**
  - Localized neural circuits
- Reusable pathways in the brain
- Long-term potentiation

The Physiology of Memory

- Anatomy
  - Anterograde and Retrograde Amnesia
- Cerebral cortex, Prefrontal cortex, Hippocampus,
- Dentate gyrus, Amygdala, Cerebellum

Are There Multiple Memory Systems?

- Declarative vs. Procedural
- Semantic vs. Episodic
- Prospective vs. Retrospective

Improving Everyday Memory

- Engage in adequate rehearsal
- Distribute practice and minimize interference
- Emphasize deep processing and transfer-appropriate processing
- Organize information
- Use verbal mnemonics
- Use visual mnemonics

Chapter 8: Language and Thought

The Cognitive Revolution

- 19th Century focus on the mind
  - Introspection

- Behaviorist focus on overt responses
  - arguments regarding incomplete picture of human functioning

- Empirical study of cognition – 1956 conference
  - **Simon and Newell** – problem solving
  - **Chomsky** – new model of language
  - **Miller** – memory

Language: Turning Thoughts into Words

- Properties of Language
  - Symbolic
  - Semantic
  - Generative
  - Structured

The Hierarchical Structure of Language

- **Phonemes** = smallest speech units
  - 100 possible, English – about 40

- **Morphemes** = smallest unit of meaning
  - 50,000 in English, root words, prefixes, suffixes

- **Semantics** = meaning of words and word combinations
  - Objects and actions to which words refer

- **Syntax** = a system of rules for arranging words into sentences
  - Different rules for different languages

Language Development: Milestones

- Initial vocalizations similar across languages
  - Crying, cooing, babbling

- **6 months** – babbling sounds begin to resemble surrounding language

- **1 year** – first word
  - similar cross-culturally – words for parents
  - receptive vs. expressive language

Language Development:
Milestones Continued

- **18-24 months** – vocabulary spurt
  - fast mapping
  - over and underextensions

- End of second year – combine words
  - Telegraphic speech
  - Mean Length of Utterance (MLU)

- **End of third year** – complex ideas, plural, past tense
  - Overregularization

Bilingualism:
Learning More Than One Language

- Research findings:
  - Smaller vocabularies in one language, combined vocabularies average
  - Higher scores for middle-class bilingual subjects on cognitive flexibility, analytical reasoning, selective attention, and metalinguistic awareness
  - Slight disadvantage in terms of language processing speed
  - 2nd languages more easily acquired early in life
  - Greater acculturation facilitates acquisition

Can Animals Develop Language?

- Dolphins, sea lions, parrots, chimpanzees
  - Vocal apparatus issue
  - American Sign Language

- Allen and Beatrice Gardner (1969)
  - Chimpanzee - Washoe
  - 160 word vocabulary

- Sue Savage-Rumbaugh
  - Bonobo chimpanzee - Kanzi
  - Symbols
  - Receptive language – 72% of 660 requests

Theories of Language Acquisition

- Behaviorist
  - Skinner

- learning of specific verbal responses

- **Nativist**
  - Chomsky

- learning the rules of language

- Language Acquisition Device (LAD)

- **Interactionist**
  - Cognitive, social communication, and emergentist theories

Problem Solving: Types of Problems

- Greeno (1978) – three basic classes

- Problems of inducing structure
  - Series completion and analogy problems

- Problems of arrangement
  - String problem and Anagrams

- Often solved through insight

- Problems of transformation
  - Hobbits and orcs problem
  - Water jar problem

Effective Problem Solving

- Well defined vs. ill defined problems

- Barriers to effective problem solving:
  - Irrelevant Information
  - Functional Fixedness
  - Mental Set
  - Unnecessary Constraints

Approaches to Problem Solving

- Algorithms
  - Systematic trial-and-error
  - Guaranteed solution

- Heuristics
  - Shortcuts
  - No guaranteed solution

- Forming subgoals

- Working backward

- Searching for analogies

- Changing the representation of a problem

Culture, Cognitive Style, and Problem Solving

- Field dependence – relying on external frames of reference

- Field independence – relying on internal frames of reference
  - Western cultures inspire field independence
  - Cultural influence based in ecological demands

- Holistic vs. analytic cognitive styles

Decision Making:
Evaluating Alternatives and Making Choices

- **Simon (1957)** – theory of bounded rationality
- Making Choices
  - Additive strategies
  - Elimination by aspects
  - Risky decision making
- Expected value
- Subjective utility
- Subjective probability

Heuristics in Judging Probabilities

- The availability heuristic
- The representativeness heuristic
- The tendency to ignore base rates
- The conjunction fallacy
- The alternative outcomes effect

Understanding Pitfalls in Reasoning
About Decisions

- The gambler's fallacy
- Overestimating the improbable
- Confirmation bias and belief perseverance
- The overconfidence effect
- Framing

Evolutionary Analyses: Flaws in Decision Making and
Fast and Frugal Heuristics

- Cosmides and Tooby (1996)
  - Unrealistic standard of rationality
  - Decision making evolved to handle real-world adaptive problems
  - Problem solving research based on contrived, artificial problems
- Gigerenzer (2000)
  - Quick and dirty heuristics
  - Less than perfect but adaptive

Chapter 9: Intelligence and Psychological Testing

Principle Types of Psychological Tests

- Mental ability tests
  - Intelligence – general
  - Aptitude – specific
- Personality scales
  - Measure motives, interests, values, and attitudes

Key Concepts in Psychological Testing

- Standardization
  - Test norms
  - Standardization group
- Reliability
  - Correlation coefficient
- Validity
  - Content validity
  - Criterion-related validity
  - Construct validity

The Evolution of Intelligence Testing

- Sir Francis Galton (1869)
  - Hereditary Genius
- Alfred Binet and Theodore Simon (1905)
  - Binet-Simon Intelligence Scale
  - Mental age
- Lewis Terman (1916)
  - Stanford-Binet Intelligence Scale
  - Intelligence Quotient (IQ) = MA/CA x 100
- David Wechsler (1955)
  - Wechsler Adult Intelligence Scale

Reliability and Validity of IQ tests

- **Exceptionally reliable** – correlations into the .90s
- **Qualified validity** – valid indicators of academic/verbal intelligence, not intelligence in a truly general sense
  - Correlations:
  - .40s–.50s with school success
  - .60s–.80s with number of years in school
- Predictive of occupational attainment, debate about predictiveness of performance

Extremes of Intelligence: Mental Retardation

- Diagnosis based on IQ and adaptive testing
  - IQ 2 or more SD below mean
  - Adaptive skill deficits
  - Origination before age 18
- 4 levels: mild, moderate, severe, profound
  - Mild most common by far
- Causes:
  - Environmental vs. biological

Extremes of Intelligence: Giftedness

- **Identification issues** – ideals vs. practice
  - IQ 2 SD above mean standard
  - Creativity, leadership, special talent?
- **Stereotypes** – weak, socially inept, emotionally troubled
  - Lewis Terman (1925) – largely contradicted stereotypes
  - Ellen Winner (1997) – moderately vs. profoundly gifted

Extremes of Intelligence: Giftedness

- Giftedness and high achievement – beyond IQ
  - Renzulli (2002) – intersection of three factors
  - Simonton (2001) – drudge theory and inborn talent

Intelligence: Heredity or Environment?

- Heredity
  - Family and twin studies
  - Heritability estimates
- Environment
  - Adoption studies
  - Cumulative deprivation hypothesis
  - The Flynn effect
- Interaction
  - The concept of the reaction range

Cultural Differences in IQ

- **Heritability** as an Explanation
  - Aurthur Jensen (1969)
  - Herrnstein and Murray (1994) – *The Bell Curve*
- **Environment** as an Explanation
  - **Kamin**'s cornfield analogy – socioeconomic disadvantage
  - **Steele (1997)** - stereotype vulnerability

New Directions in the Study of Intelligence

- Biological Indexes and Correlates of Intelligence
  - Reaction time and inspection time
  - Brain size
- Cognitive Conceptualizations of Intelligence
  - Sternberg's triarchic theory and successful intelligence
- Expanding the Concept of Intelligence
  - Gardner's multiple intelligences
  - Goleman's emotional intelligence

_____

_____

_____

_____

_____

_____

_____

Chapter 10: Motivation and Emotion

Motivational Theories and Concepts

- **Motives** – needs, wants, desires leading to goal-directed behavior

- **Drive theories** – seeking homeostasis

- **Incentive theories** – regulation by external stimuli

- **Evolutionary theories** – maximizing reproductive success

The Motivation of Hunger and Eating: Biological Factors

- Brain regulation
  - Lateral and ventromedial hypothalamus
  - Paraventricular nucleus

- Glucose and digestive regulation
  - Glucostatic theory

- Hormonal regulation
  - Insulin and leptin

The Motivation of Hunger and Eating: Environmental Factors

- Learned preferences and habits
  - Exposure
  - When, as well as what

- Food-related cues
  - Appearance, odor, effort required

- Stress
  - Link between heightened arousal/negative emotion and overeating

Eating and Weight: The Roots of Obesity

- Evolutionary explanations

- Genetic predisposition
  - Body Mass Index and adoption study

- The concept of set point/settling point

- Dietary restraint

_____
_____
_____
_____
_____
_____
_____
_____
_____
_____
_____
_____
_____
_____
_____
_____
_____
_____
_____
_____
_____
_____
_____
_____

Sexual Motivation and Behavior: Determining Desire

- Hormonal regulation
  - Estrogens
  - Androgens
  - Testosterone

- Pheromones
  - Synchronized menstrual cycles

- Aphrodisiacs

- Erotic materials

- Attraction to a Partner

- The Coolidge effect

- Evolutionary factors

The Mystery of Sexual Orientation

- Heterosexual – Bisexual – Homosexual
  - A continuum

- Theories explaining homosexuality
  - Environmental
  - Biological
  - Interactionist

The Human Sexual Response

- Masters and Johnson – 1966

- Stages:
  - Excitement
  - Plateau
  - Orgasm
  - Resolution

Achievement Motivation

- Achievement motive = need to excel
  - Work harder and more persistently
  - Delay gratification
  - Pursue competitive careers
  - Situational influences on achievement motives
  - Thematic Apperception Test (TAT)

The Elements of Emotional Experience

- Cognitive component
  - Subjective conscious experience
  - Positive psychology

- Physiological component
  - Bodily (autonomic) arousal

- Behavioral component
  - Characteristic overt expressions

Theories of Emotion

- James-Lange
  - Feel afraid because pulse is racing
- Cannon-Bard
  - Thalamus sends signals simultaneously to the cortex and the autonomic nervous system

- Schacter's Two-Factor Theory
  - Look to external cues to decide what to feel
- Evolutionary Theories
  - Innate reactions with little cognitive interpretation

Happiness

- Common sense notions incorrect
  - Income, age, parenthood, intelligence, and attractiveness largely uncorrelated
  - Physical health, good social relationships, religious faith, and culture modestly correlated
  - Love, marriage, work satisfaction, and personality strongly correlated
- Subjective rather than objective reality important

Chapter 11: Human Development Across the Life Span

Progress Before Birth:
Prenatal Development

- 3 phases
  - **germinal stage** = first 2 weeks
  - conception, implantation, formation of placenta
  - **embryonic stage** = 2 weeks – 2 months

- formation of vital organs and systems
  - **fetal stage** = 2 months – birth

- bodily growth continues, movement capability begins, brain cells multiply

- age of viability

Environmental Factors
and Prenatal Development

- Maternal nutrition
  - Malnutrition linked to increased risk of birth complications, neurological problems, and psychopathology

- Maternal drug use
  - Tobacco, alcohol, prescription, and recreational drugs
  - Fetal alcohol syndrome

Environmental Factors
and Prenatal Development

- Maternal illness
  - Rubella, syphilis, mumps, genital herpes, AIDS, severe influenza
  - Prenatal health care
  - Prevention through guidance

The Childhood Years: Motor Development

- Basic Principles
  - Cephalocaudal trend – head to foot
  - Proximodistal trend – center-outward

- **Maturation** – gradual unfolding of genetic blueprint

- **Developmental norms** – median age
  - Cultural variations

Easy and Difficult Babies:
Differences in Temperament

- Longitudinal vs. cross-sectional designs
- **Thomas, Chess, and Birch (1970)**
  - 3 basic temperamental styles
- easy – 40%
- slow-to-warm-up – 15%
- difficult – 10%
- mixed – 35%
  - stable over time

Easy and Difficult Babies:
Differences in Temperament

- Kagan & Snidman (1991)
  - Inhibited vs. uninhibited temperament
- inhibited – 15 - 20%
- uninhibited – 25 - 30%
  - stable over time, genetically based

Early Emotional Development: Attachment

- Separation anxiety
  - Ainsworth (1979)
  - The strange situation and patterns of attachment
- Secure
- Anxious-ambivalent
- Avoidant
- Developing secure attachment
  - Bonding at birth
  - Daycare
  - Cultural factors
- Evolutionary perspectives on attachment
- Stage Theories of Development: Personality
- Stage theories, three components
  - progress through stages in order
  - progress through stages related to age
  - major discontinuities in development
- Erik Erikson (1963)
  - Eight stages spanning the lifespan
  - **Psychosocial crises** determining balance between opposing polarities in personality

Stage Theories: Cognitive Development

- Jean Piaget (1920s-1980s)
  - Assimilation/ Accommodation
  - 4 stages and major milestones
- Sensorimotor
  - Object permanence
- Preoperational
  - Centration, Egocentrism
- Concrete Operational
  - Decentration, Reversibility, Conservation
- Formal Operational
  - Abstraction

The Development of Moral Reasoning

- Kohlberg (1976)
  - Reasoning as opposed to behavior
- Moral dilemmas
  - Measured nature and progression of moral reasoning
  - 3 levels, each with 2 sublevels
- Preconventional
- Conventional
- Postconventional

Adolescence: Physiological Changes

- Pubescence
- Puberty
  - Secondary sex characteristics
  - Primary sex characteristics
- Menarche
- Sperm production
  - Maturation: early vs. late
- Sex differences in effects of early maturation

Adolescence: Neural Changes

- Increasing myelinization
- Synaptic pruning
- Changes in prefrontal cortex

The Search for Identity

- Erik Erikson (1968)
  - Key challenge - forming a sense of identity
- James Marcia (1988)
  - 4 identity statuses
- Foreclosure
- Moratorium
- Identity Diffusion
- Identity Achievement

The Expanse of Adulthood

- Personality development
- Social development
- Career development
- Physical changes
- Cognitive changes

Chapter 12: Personality: Theory, Research, and Assessment

Defining Personality:
Consistency and Distinctiveness

- Personality Traits
  - Dispositions and dimensions

- The Five-Factor Model
  - Extraversion
  - Neuroticism
  - Openness to experience
  - Agreeableness
  - Conscientiousness

Psychodynamic Perspectives

- Freud's psychoanalytic theory
  - Structure of personality

- **Id** - Pleasure principle

- **Ego** - Reality principle

- **Superego** - Morality
  - Levels of awareness
    - Conscious
    - Unconscious
    - Preconscious

Psychodynamic Perspectives

- Freud's psychoanalytic theory
  - Conflict

- Sex and Aggression

- Anxiety

- Defense Mechanisms

Freud on Development:
Psychosexual Stages

- Sexual = physical pleasure

- Psychosexual stages
  - Oral, Anal, Phallic, Latency, Genital

- Fixation = Excessive gratification or frustration

- Overemphasis on psychosexual needs during fixated stage

Other Psychodynamic Theorists

- Carl Jung: Analytical Psychology
  - Personal and collective unconscious
  - Archetypes
  - Introversion/Extroversion

- Alfred Adler: Individual Psychology
  - Striving for superiority
  - Compensation
  - Inferiority complex/overcompensation
  - Birth order

Evaluating Psychodynamic Perspectives

- Pros
  - The unconscious
  - The role of internal conflict
  - The importance of early childhood experiences

- Cons
  - Poor testability
  - Inadequate empirical base
  - Sexist views

Behavioral Perspectives

- Skinner's views
  - Conditioning and response tendencies
  - Environmental determinism

- Bandura's views
  - Social leaning theory

- Cognitive processes and reciprocal determinism

- Observational learning

- Models

- Self-efficacy

- **Mischel's views**
  - The person-situation controversy

Evaluating Behavioral Perspectives

- Pros
  - Based on rigorous research
  - Insights into effects of learning and environmental factors

- Cons
  - Over-dependence on animal research
  - Fragmented view of personality
  - Dehumanizing views

Humanistic Perspectives

- Carl Rogers
  - Person Centered Theory

- Self-concept
  - Conditional/unconditional positive regard
  - Incongruence and anxiety

- Abraham Maslow
  - Self-actualization theory
  - Hierarchy of needs

- The healthy personality

Evaluating Humanistic Perspectives

- Humanistic theories are credited with highlighting the importance of a person's subjective view of reality. They are also applauded for focusing attention on the issue of what constitutes a healthy personality.

- They are criticized for lacking a strong research base, poor testability, and what may be an overly optimistic view of human nature (Maslow had a hard time finding live people who had self-actualized).

Biological Perspectives

- Eysenk's theory
  - 3 higher order traits
  - Extraversion, neuroticism, and psychoticism

- Determined by genes

- Twin studies
  - Novelty seeking and genetics

- The evolutionary approach
  - Traits conducive to reproductive fitness

Evaluating Biological Perspectives

- Pros
  - Convincing evidence for genetic influence

- Cons
  - Conceptual problems with heritability estimates
  - Artificial carving apart of nature and nurture
  - No comprehensive biological theory

Contemporary Empirical Approaches: Terror Management Theory

- Conflict between self-preservation and ability to foresee death

- Culture and self-esteem

- Anxiety buffer

Contemporary Empirical Approaches:
Terror Management Theory

- Increasing subjects' mortality salience causes them to:
  - Punish moral transgressions more harshly
  - Be less tolerant of criticism of their country
  - Give greater rewards to those who uphold cultural standards
  - Respect cultural icons more

_____

_____

_____

_____

_____

Chapter 13: Stress, Coping, and Health

**The Relationship
Between Stress and Disease**

- Contagious diseases vs. chronic diseases
  - Biopsychosocial model
  - Health psychology

- Health promotion and maintenance
  - Discovery of causation, prevention, and treatment

Stress: An Everyday Event

- Major stressors vs. routine hassles
  - Cumulative nature of stress
  - Cognitive appraisals

Major Types of Stress

- **Frustration**: blocked goal

- **Conflict**: incompatible motivations
  - Approach-approach
  - Approach-avoidance
  - Avoidance-avoidance

- **Change:** having to adapt
  - Social Readjustment Rating Scale
  - Life Change Units

- Pressure
  - Perform/conform

Responding to Stress Emotionally

- Emotional Responses
  - Annoyance, anger, rage
  - Apprehension, anxiety, fear
  - Dejection, sadness, grief
  - Positive emotions

- Emotional response and performance
  - The inverted-U-hypothesis

Responding to Stress Physiologically

- Physiological Responses
  - Fight-or-flight response
  - Selye's General Adaptation Syndrome

- Alarm

- Resistance

- Exhaustion

Responding to Stress Behaviorally

- Behavioral Responses
  - Frustration-aggression hypothesis
  - catharsis
  - defense mechanisms

- Coping

**Effects of Stress:
Behavioral and Psychological**

- Impaired task performance

- Burnout

- Psychological problems and disorders

- Positive effects

Effects of Stress: Physical

- Psychosomatic diseases

- Heart disease
  - Type A behavior - 3 elements

- strong competitiveness

- impatience and time urgency

- anger and hostility
  - Emotional reactions and depression

- Stress and immune functioning
  - Reduced immune activity

Factors Moderating the Impact of Stress

- Social support
  - Increased immune functioning

- Optimism
  - More adaptive coping
  - Pessimistic explanatory style

- Conscientiousness
  - Fostering better health habits

- Autonomic reactivity
  - Cardiovascular reactivity to stress

Health-Impairing Behaviors

- Smoking

- Poor nutrition

- Lack of exercise

- Alcohol and drug use

- Risky sexual behavior

- Transmission, misconceptions, and prevention of AIDS

Reactions to Illness

- Seeking treatment
  - Ignoring physical symptoms

- Communication with health care providers
  - Barriers to effective communication

- Following medical advice
  - Noncompliance

_____

_____

_____

_____

_____

_____

_____

_____

_____

_____

_____

Chapter 14: Psychological Disorders

Abnormal Behavior

- The medical model

- What is abnormal behavior?
  - Deviant
  - Maladaptive
  - Causing personal distress

- A continuum of normal/abnormal

Prevalence, Causes, and Course

- Epidemiology

- Prevalence

- Lifetime prevalence

- Diagnosis

- Etiology

- Prognosis

Psychodiagnosis:
The Classification of Disorders

- American Psychiatric Association

- *Diagnostic and Statistical Manual of Mental Disorders –* 4th ed. (DSM - 4)

Five Axes

- Axis I – Clinical Syndromes

- Axis II – Personality Disorders or Mental Retardation

- Axis III – General Medical Conditions

- Axis IV – Psychosocial and Environmental Problems

- Axis V – Global Assessment of Functioning

Axis I Clinical Syndromes

- Anxiety Disorders

- Somatoform Disorders

- Dissociative Disorders

- Mood Disorders

- Schizophrenic Disorders

Clinical Syndromes: Anxiety Disorders

- Generalized anxiety disorder
  - "free-floating anxiety"
- Phobic disorder
  - Specific focus of fear
- Panic disorder and agoraphobia
- Obsessive compulsive disorder
  - Obsessions
  - Compulsions
- Posttraumatic Stress Disorder

Etiology of Anxiety Disorders

- Biological factors
  - Genetic predisposition, anxiety sensitivity
  - GABA circuits in the brain
- Conditioning and learning
  - Acquired through classical conditioning or observational learning
  - Maintained through operant conditioning
- Cognitive factors
  - Judgments of perceived threat
- Personality
  - Neuroticism
- Stress—a precipitator

Clinical Syndromes: Somatoform Disorders

- Somatization Disorder
- Conversion Disorder
- Hypochondriasis
  - Etiology
- Reactive autonomic nervous system
- Personality factors
- Cognitive factors
- The sick role

Clinical Syndromes: Dissociative Disorders

- Dissociative amnesia
- Dissociative fugue
- Dissociative identity disorder
  - Etiology
- severe emotional trauma during childhood
  - Controversy

- Media creation?

Clinical Syndromes: Mood Disorders

- Major depressive disorder
  - Dysthymic disorder

- Bipolar disorder
  - Cyclothymic disorder

- Etiology
  - Genetic vulnerability
  - Neurochemical factors
  - Cognitive factors
  - Interpersonal roots
  - Precipitating stress

Clinical Syndromes: Schizophrenia

- General symptoms
  - Delusions and irrational thought
  - Deterioration of adaptive behavior
  - Hallucinations
  - Disturbed emotions

- Prognostic factors

Subtyping of Schizophrenia

- 4 subtypes
  - Paranoid type
  - Catatonic type
  - Disorganized type
  - Undifferentiated type

- New model for classification
  - Positive vs. negative symptoms

Etiology of Schizophrenia

- Genetic vulnerability

- Neurochemical factors

- Structural abnormalities of the brain

- The neurodevelopmental hypothesis

- Expressed emotion

- Precipitating stress

Personality Disorders

- Anxious-fearful cluster
  - Avoidant, dependent, obsessive-compulsive
- Dramatic-impulsive cluster
  - Histrionic, narcissistic, borderline, antisocial
- Odd-eccentric cluster
  - Schizoid, schizotypal, paranoid
- Etiology
  - Genetic predispositions, inadequate socialization in dysfunctional families

Psychological Disorders and the Law

- Insanity
  - M'naghten rule
- Involuntary commitment
  - danger to self
  - danger to others
  - in need of treatment

Culture and Pathology

- Cultural variations
- Culture bound disorders
  - Koro
  - Windigo
  - Anorexia nervosa

Chapter 15: Treatment of Psychological Disorders

Types of Treatment

- Psychotherapy
  - Insight therapies
- "Talk therapy"
  - Behavior therapies
- Changing overt behavior
  - Biomedical therapies
- Biological functioning interventions

Who Seeks Treatment?

- 15% of U.S. population in a given year
- Most common presenting problems
  - Anxiety and Depression
- Women more than men
- Medical insurance
- Education level

Who Provides Treatment?

- Clinical psychologists
- Counseling psychologists
- Psychiatrists
- Clinical social workers
- Psychiatric nurses
- Counselors

Insight Therapies: Psychoanalysis

- **Sigmund Freud** and followers
  - Goal: discover unresolved unconscious conflicts
- Free association
- Dream analysis
- Interpretation
  - Resistance and transference

Insight Therapies: Client-Centered Therapy

- Carl Rogers
  - Goal: restructure self-concept to better correspond to reality
  - Therapeutic Climate
- Genuineness
- Unconditional positive regard
- Empathy

Behavior Therapies

- **B.F. Skinner** and colleagues
  - Goal: unlearning maladaptive behavior and learning adaptive ones
  - **Systematic Desensitization – Joseph Wolpe**

- Classical conditioning

- Anxiety hierarchy
  - Aversion therapy

- Alcoholism, sexual deviance, smoking, etc.

Behavior Therapy

- **B.F. Skinner** and colleagues
  - Social skills training

- Modeling

- Behavioral rehearsal

Cognitive-Behavioral Therapy

- Aaron Beck
  - Cognitive therapy

- Goal: to change the way clients think
  - Detect and recognize negative thoughts
  - Reality testing
  - Kinship with behavior therapy

Biomedical Therapies

- Psychopharmacotherapy
  - Antianxiety - Valium, Xanax, Buspar
  - Antipsychotic - Thorazine, Mellaril, Haldol

- Tardive dyskinesia

- Clozapine
  - Antidepressant:

- Tricyclics – Elavil, Tofranil

- Mao inhibitors (MAOIs) - Nardil

- Selective serotonin reuptake inhibitors (SSRIs) – Prozac, Paxil, Zoloft

Biomedical Therapies

- Psychopharmacotherapy
  - Mood stabilizers

- Lithium

- Valproic acid

- Electroconvulsive therapy (ECT)

Current Trends and Issues in Treatment

- Managed care

- Empirically validated treatments

- Blending Approaches to treatment

- Multicultural sensitivity

- Deinstitutionalization
  - Revolving door problem
  - Homelessness

_____

_____

_____

_____

_____

_____

Chapter 16: Social Behavior

Social Psychology

- Person perception
- Attribution processes
- Interpersonal attraction
- Attitudes
- Conformity and obedience
- Behavior in groups

Person Perception:
Forming Impressions of Others

- Effects of physical appearance
- Cognitive schemas
- Stereotypes
- Prejudice and discrimination
- Subjectivity in person perception
- Evolutionary perspectives

Attribution Processes: Explaining Behavior

- Attributions
  - Internal vs. External
  - Kelley's covariation model
- Biases in attributions
  - Fundamental attribution error
  - Defensive attribution
  - Self-serving bias
- Cultural influences

Close Relationships: Liking and Loving

- Key factors in attraction
  - Physical attractiveness
  - Matching hypothesis
  - Similarity
  - Reciprocity
  - Romantic Ideals

Close Relationships: Liking and Loving

- Perspectives on love
  - Hatfield & Berscheid – Passionate vs. Companionate love
  - Sternberg - Intimacy and commitment
  - Hazen & Shaver – Love as attachment

- Evolutionary perspectives
  - Mating priorities

Attitudes and Attitude Change

- 3 components
  - cognitive, affective, and behavioral
- Factors in changing attitudes
  - source, message, and receiver
- Theories of attitude change
  - Learning theory
  - Dissonance theory
  - Self-perception theory
  - Elaboration likelihood model

Yielding to Others: Conformity

- Conformity – Solomon Asch (1950s)
  - Classic experiment
- Group size
- Group unanimity

Yielding to Others: Obedience

- Obedience – Stanley Milgram (1960s)
  - Controversial landmark experiment
  - "I was just following orders"
- Presence of a dissenter

**Behavior in Groups:
The Influence of Other People**

- The bystander effect - Darley and Latane (1968)
- Diffusion of responsibility
- Group productivity and social loafing
- Decision making in groups
- Polarization
- Groupthink

Appendix B: Statistical Methods

Statistical Methods: Graphing Data

- Frequency distribution

- Histogram

- Frequency polygon

Descriptive Statistics

- Measures of Central Tendency

- Mean

- Median

- Mode

- Skewed Distributions

- Negative/Positive

- Measuring Variability

- Standard Deviation

The Normal Distribution

- Psychological tests
  - Relative measures
  - Standard deviation the unit of measure

- Conversion to percentile scores

Measuring Correlation

- Correlation coefficient
  - Positive = direct relationship
  - Negative = inverse relationship

- Magnitude: 0 to plus/minus 1

- Scatter diagrams

- Correlation of determination

Hypothesis Testing

- Inferential statistics

- Sample

- Population

- Null hypothesis vs. research hypothesis

- Statistical significance

_____

_____

_____

_____

_____

_____

_____

_____

_____

_____

_____

_____

_____

_____

_____

_____

_____

_____

_____

_____

_____

_____

_____

_____

_____

_____

Appendix C: Industrial/Organizational Psychology

Industrial Psychology

- Recruitment
- Selection
- Employment discrimination
- Training
- Performance appraisal

Organizational Psychology

- Organizational culture
- Work teams
- Psychological contracts
- Work motivation
- Leadership

_____

_____

_____

_____

_____

_____

_____

_____

_____

_____

Appendix C: Careers in Psychology

With a Major

- A psychology major is excellent preparation for a wide range of entry-level positions
- Starting salaries
- Developing skills
    - College classes
    - Relevant work experience
    - Extracurricular activities

With a Master's Degree

- Clinical psychology
- Clinical social work
- Agency counseling

With a Doctorate

- Teaching and research
- Applied work

_____

_____

_____

_____

_____

_____

_____

_____

_____

Figure 1
Major research areas in contemporary psychology
Fill in the table with the appropriate terms.

Area	Focus of research
_____ psychology	Looks at human development across the life span. Developmental psychology once focused primarily on child development, but today devotes a great deal of research to adolescence, adulthood, and old age.
_____ psychology	Focuses on interpersonal behavior and the role of social forces in governing behavior. Typical topics include attitude formation, attitude change, prejudice, conformity, attraction, aggression, intimate relationships, and behavior in groups.
_____ psychology	Encompasses the traditional core of topics that psychology focused on heavily in its first half-century as a science: sensation, perception, learning, conditioning, motivation, and emotion. The name experimental psychology is somewhat misleading, as this is not the only area in which experiments are done. Psychologists working in all the areas listed here conduct experiments.
_____ psychology	Examines the influence of genetic factors on behavior and the role of the brain, nervous system, endocrine system, and bodily chemicals in the regulation of behavior.
_____ psychology	Focuses on "higher" mental processes, such as memory, reasoning, information processing, language, problem solving, decision making, and creativity.
_____	Is interested in describing and understanding individuals' consistency in behavior, which represents their personality. This area of interest is also concerned with the factors that shape personality and with personality assessment.
_____	Is concerned with the measurement of behavior and capacities, usually through the development of psychological tests. Psychometrics is involved with the design of tests to assess personality, intelligence, and a wide range of abilities. It is also concerned with the development of new techniques for statistical analysis.

Notes:

_____

_____

_____

_____

_____

_____

_____

_____

Refer to page 20 in your text for correct answers

Figure 2
Principle professional specialties in contemporary psychology

Fill in the table with the appropriate terms.

Specialty	Focus of professional practice
_____ psychology	Clinical psychologists are concerned with the evaluation, diagnosis, and treatment of individuals with psychological disorders, as well as treatment of less severe behavioral and emotional problems. Principal activities include interviewing clients, psychological testing, and providing group or individual psychotherapy.
_____ psychology	Counseling psychology overlaps with clinical psychology in that specialists in both areas engage in similar activities—interviewing, testing, and providing therapy. However, counseling psychologists usually work with a somewhat different clientele, providing assistance to people struggling with everyday problems of moderate severity. Thus, they often specialize in family, marital, or career counseling.
_____ and school psychology	Educational psychologists work to improve curriculum design, achievement testing, teacher training, and other aspects of the educational process. School psychologists usually work in elementary or secondary schools, where they test and counsel children having difficulties in school and aid parents and teachers in solving school-related problems.
_____ and _____ psychology	Psychologists in this area perform a wide variety of tasks in the world of business and industry. These tasks include running human resources departments, working to improve staff morale and attitudes, striving to increase job satisfaction and productivity, examining organizational structures and procedures, and making recommendations for improvements.

Notes:

_____

_____

_____

_____

_____

_____

_____

_____

_____

Refer to page 20 in your text for correct answers

Figure 3
Structure of the neuron
Fill in the diagram with the appropriate terms.

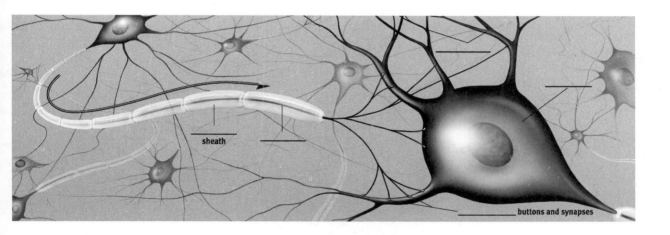

Notes:

_____

_____

_____

_____

_____

_____

_____

_____

Refer to page 74 in your text for correct answers

Figure 4
The synapse
Fill in the diagram with the appropriate terms.

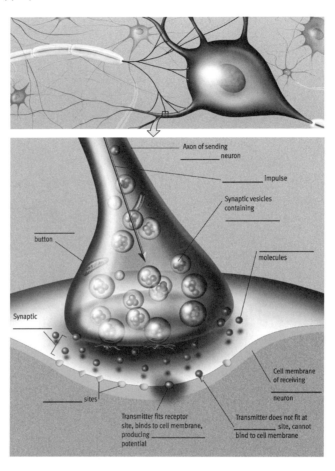

Notes:

_____

_____

_____

_____

_____

_____

_____

_____

Refer to page 77 in your text for correct answers

Figure 5
Overview of synaptic transmission
Fill in the diagram with the appropriate terms.

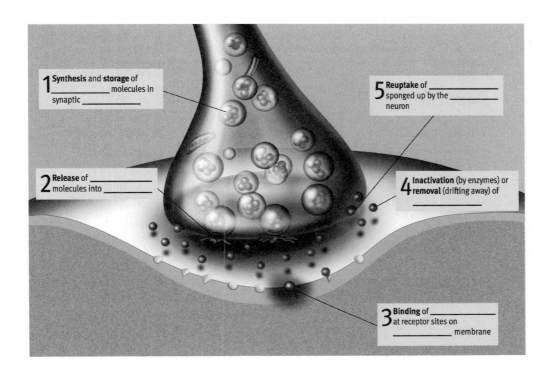

1 **Synthesis** and **storage** of _____ molecules in synaptic _____

2 **Release** of _____ molecules into _____

3 **Binding** of _____ at receptor sites on _____ membrane

4 **Inactivation** (by enzymes) or **removal** (drifting away) of _____

5 **Reuptake** of _____ sponged up by the _____ neuron

Notes:

_____

_____

_____

_____

_____

_____

_____

_____

_____

Refer to page 78 in your text for correct answers

Figure 6
Common Neurotransmitters and Some of Their Functions
Fill in the table with the appropriate terms.

Table 3.1 Common Neurotransmitters and Some of Their Functions

Neurotransmitter	Functions and Characteristics
_____ (ACh)	Released by motor neurons controlling skeletal muscles Contributes to the regulation of attention, arousal, and memory Some ACh receptors stimulated by nicotine
Dopamine _____	Contributes to control of voluntary movement, pleasurable emotions Decreased levels associated with Parkinson's disease Overactivity at DA synapses associated with schizophrenia Cocaine and amphetamines elevate activity at DA synapses
_____ (NE)	Contributes to modulation of mood and arousal Cocaine and amphetamines elevate activity at NE synapses
_____	Involved in regulation of sleep and wakefulness, eating, aggression Abnormal levels may contribute to depression and obsessive-compulsive disorder Prozac and similar antidepressant drugs affect serotonin circuits
_____	Serves as widely distributed inhibitory transmitter Valium and similar antianxiety drugs work at GABA synapses
_____	Resemble opiate drugs in structure and effects Contribute to pain relief and perhaps to some pleasurable emotions

Notes:

_____

_____

_____

_____

_____

_____

_____

_____

Refer to page 79 in your text for correct answers

Figure 7
Organization of the human nervous system
Fill in the diagram with the appropriate terms.

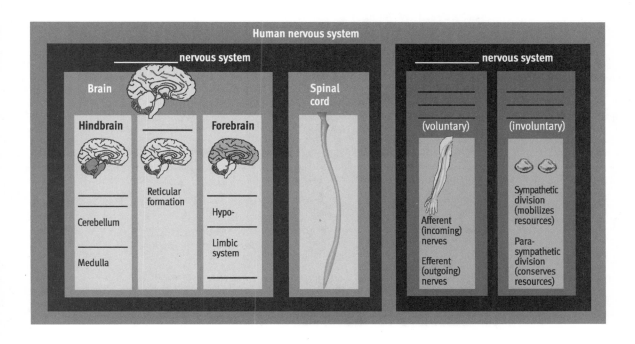

Notes:

_____

_____

_____

_____

_____

_____

_____

_____

Refer to page 82 in your text for correct answers

Figure 8
The autonomic nervous system (ANS)
Fill in the diagram with the appropriate terms.

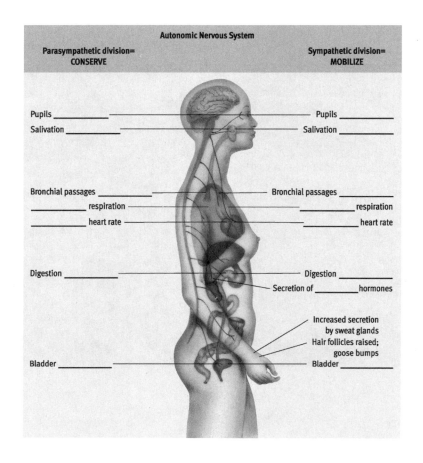

Notes:

_____

_____

_____

_____

_____

_____

_____

_____

_____

Refer to page 83 in your text for correct answers

Figure 9
Structures and areas in the human brain

Fill in the diagram with the appropriate terms.

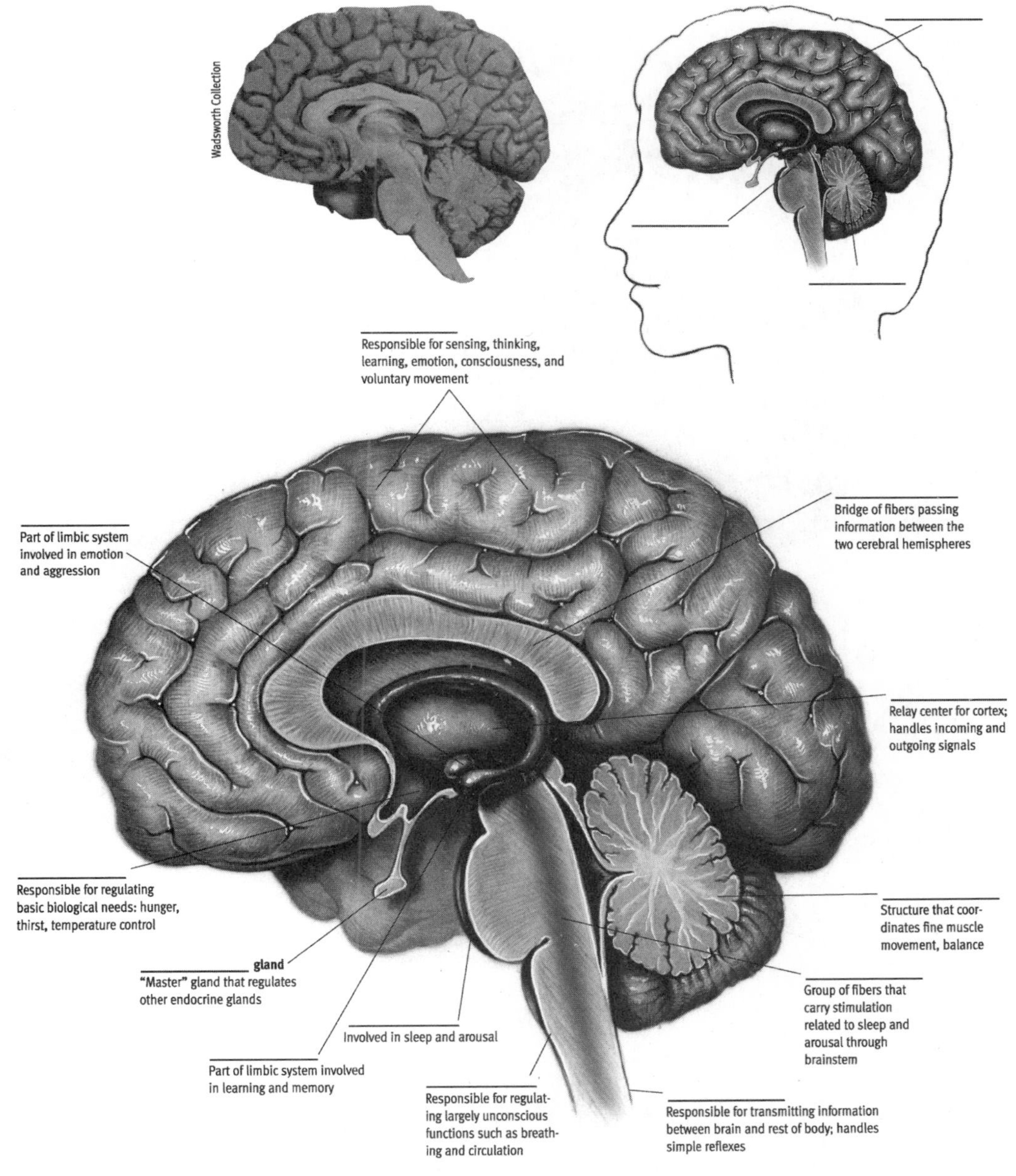

Wadsworth Collection

Responsible for sensing, thinking, learning, emotion, consciousness, and voluntary movement

Part of limbic system involved in emotion and aggression

Bridge of fibers passing information between the two cerebral hemispheres

Relay center for cortex; handles incoming and outgoing signals

Responsible for regulating basic biological needs: hunger, thirst, temperature control

_____ gland
"Master" gland that regulates other endocrine glands

Involved in sleep and arousal

Part of limbic system involved in learning and memory

Responsible for regulating largely unconscious functions such as breathing and circulation

Structure that coordinates fine muscle movement, balance

Group of fibers that carry stimulation related to sleep and arousal through brainstem

Responsible for transmitting information between brain and rest of body; handles simple reflexes

Notes:

_____

_____

_____

_____

Refer to page 91 in your text for correct answers

Figure 10
The cerebral cortex in humans
Fill in the diagram with the appropriate terms.

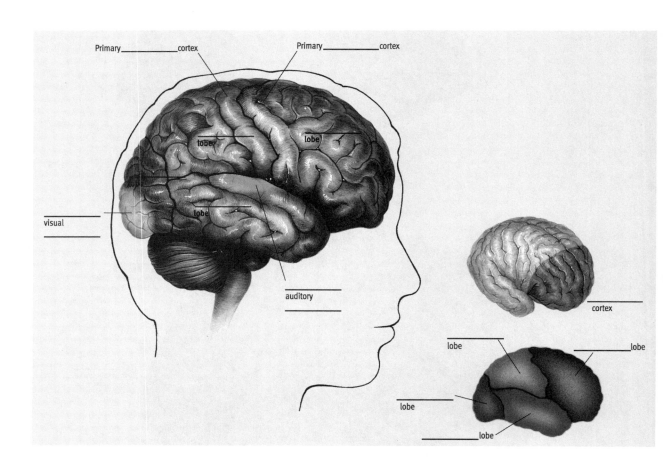

Notes:

_____

_____

_____

_____

_____

_____

_____

_____

_____

Figure 11
The endocrine system
Fill in the diagram with the appropriate terms.

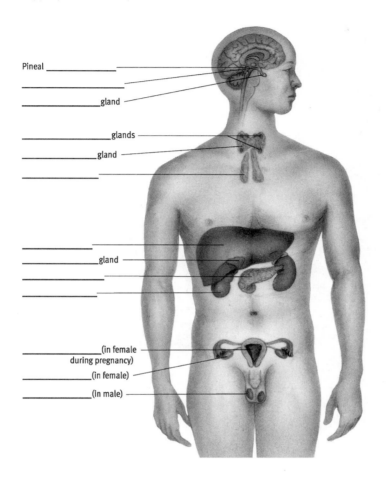

Pineal _____

_____

_____gland

_____glands

_____gland

_____

_____

_____gland

_____

_____

_____(in female during pregnancy)

_____(in female)

_____(in male)

Notes:

_____

_____

_____

_____

_____

_____

_____

_____

Refer to page 100 in your text for correct answers

Figure 12
The human eye
Fill in the diagram with the appropriate terms.

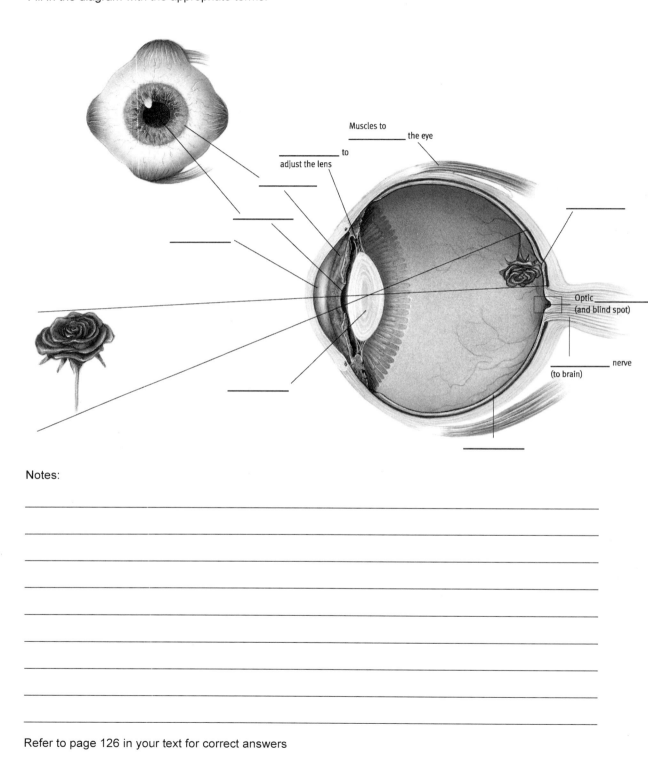

Muscles to
_____ the eye

_____ to
adjust the lens

_____

_____

_____

_____

Optic _____
(and blind spot)

_____ nerve
(to brain)

_____

Notes:

_____

_____

_____

_____

_____

_____

_____

_____

_____

Refer to page 126 in your text for correct answers

Figure 13
The retina

Fill in the diagram with the appropriate terms.

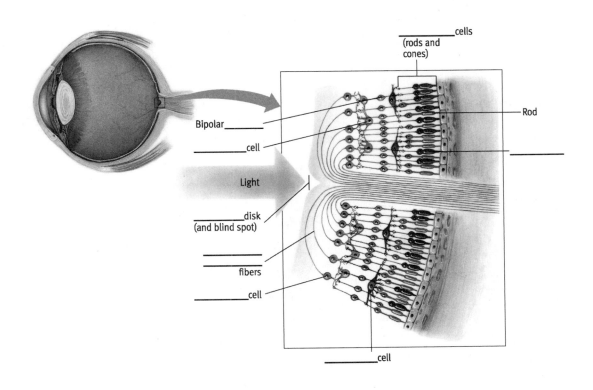

_____ cells (rods and cones)

Bipolar _____

_____ cell

Rod

Light

_____ disk (and blind spot)

_____

_____ fibers

_____ cell

_____ cell

Notes:

Refer to page 127 in your text for correct answers

Figure 14
Visual pathways through the brain
Fill in the diagram with the appropriate terms.

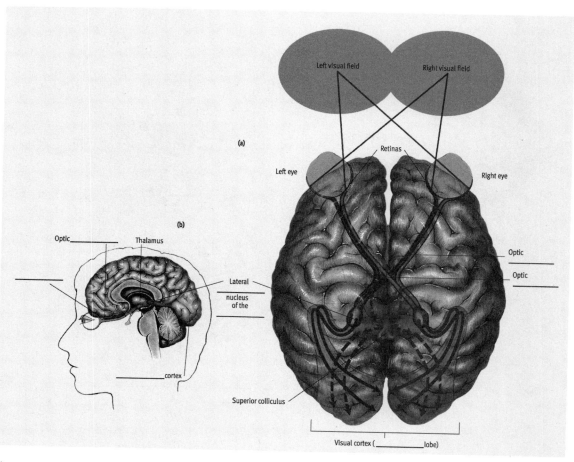

Notes:

_____

_____

_____

_____

_____

_____

_____

_____

_____

Refer to page 131 in your text for correct answers

Figure 15
The *what* and *where* pathways from the primary visual cortex
Fill in the diagram with the appropriate terms.

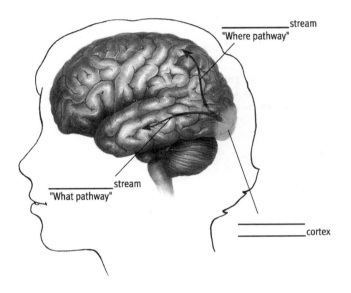

_____ stream
"Where pathway"

_____ stream
"What pathway"

_____ cortex

Notes:

_____

_____

_____

_____

_____

_____

_____

_____

_____

Refer to page 132 in your text for correct answers

Figure 16
The human ear

Fill in the diagram with the appropriate terms.

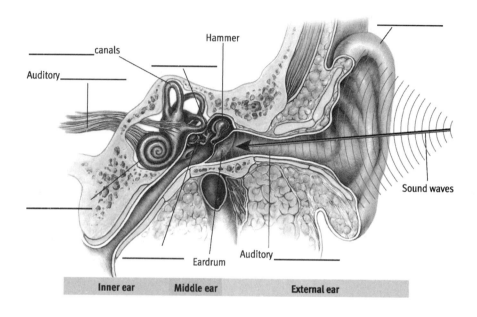

canals

Auditory_____

Hammer

Sound waves

Eardrum

Auditory_____

Inner ear	Middle ear	External ear

Notes:

_____

_____

_____

_____

_____

_____

_____

_____

Refer to page 151 in your text for correct answers

Figure 17
The tongue and taste
Fill in the diagram with the appropriate terms.

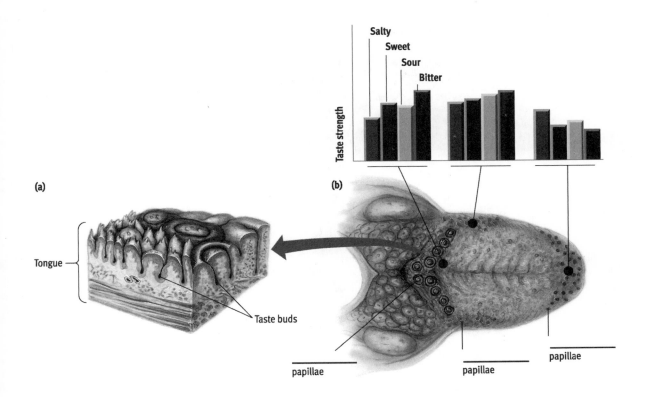

(a)

Tongue

Taste buds

(b)

Salty
Sweet
Sour
Bitter

Taste strength

papillae

papillae

papillae

Notes:

_____

_____

_____

_____

_____

_____

_____

_____

_____

Refer to page 155 in your text for correct answers

Figure 18
The olfactory system
Fill in the diagram with the appropriate terms.

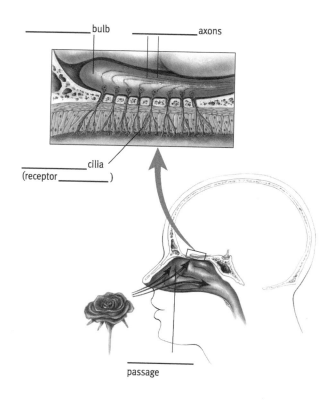

_____ bulb   _____ axons

_____ cilia
(receptor_____)

passage

Notes:

_____

_____

_____

_____

_____

_____

_____

_____

_____

Refer to page 157 in your text for correct answers

Figure 19
Pathways for pain signals

Fill in the diagram with the appropriate terms.

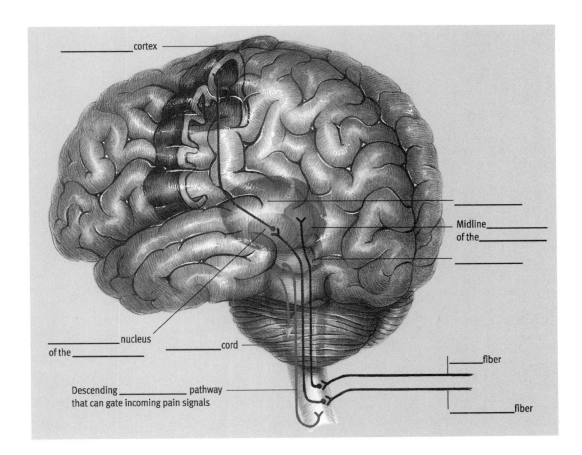

_____cortex _____

_____

Midline_____
of the_____

_____

_____nucleus
of the_____   _____cord

_____fiber

Descending_____pathway
that can gate incoming pain signals

_____fiber

Notes:

_____

_____

_____

_____

_____

_____

_____

_____

_____

Refer to page 159 in your text for correct answers

Figure 20
The ascending reticular activating system (ARAS)

Fill in the diagram with the appropriate terms.

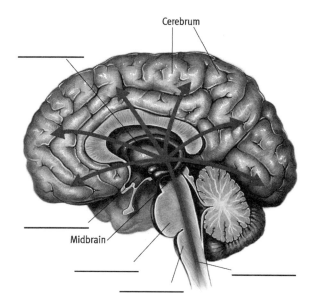

Cerebrum

Midbrain

Notes:

_____

_____

_____

_____

_____

_____

_____

_____

_____

Refer to page 183 in your text for correct answers

Figure 21
Comparison of Basic Processes in Classical and Operant Conditioning

Fill in the table with the appropriate terms.

Table 6.1 Comparison of Basic Processes in Classical and Operant Conditioning

Process and Definition	Description in Classical Conditioning	Description in Operant Conditioning
_____: The initial stage of learning	___ and ___ are paired, gradually resulting in ___.	Responding gradually increases because of reinforcement, possibly through shaping.
_____: The gradual weakening and disappearance of a conditioned response tendency	CS is presented alone until it no longer elicits ___	Responding gradually slows and stops after reinforcement is terminated.
Stimulus _____: An organism's responding to stimuli other than the original stimulus used in conditioning	___ is elicited by new stimulus that resembles original CS.	Responding increases in the presence of new stimulus that resembles original discriminative stimulus.
Stimulus _____: An organism's lack of response to stimuli that are similar to the original stimulus used in conditioning	CR is not elicited by new stimulus that resembles original ___	Responding does not increase in the presence of new stimulus that resembles original discriminative stimulus.

Notes:

_____

_____

_____

_____

_____

_____

_____

_____

Refer to page 230 in your text for correct answers

Figure 22
Levels-of-processing theory

Fill in the table with the appropriate terms.

	Level of processing	Type of encoding	Example of questions used to elicit appropriate encoding
Depth of processing	_____ processing	*Structural encoding:* emphasizes the physical structure of the stimulus	Is the word written in capital letters?
	Intermediate processing	_____*encoding:* emphasizes what a word sounds like	Does the word rhyme with weight?
	_____ processing	*Semantic encoding:* emphasizes the meaning of verbal input	Would the word fit in the sentence: "He met a _____ on the street"?

Notes:

_____

_____

_____

_____

_____

_____

_____

_____

Refer to page 261 in your text for correct answers

Figure 23
The anatomy of memory
Fill in the diagram with the appropriate terms.

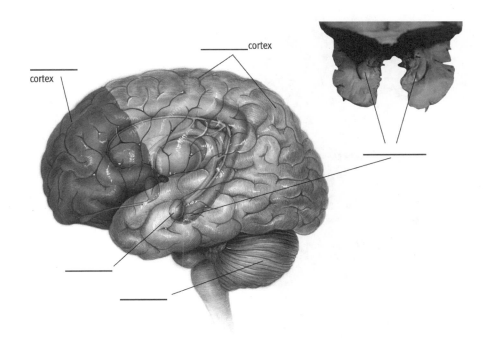

_____ cortex

cortex

Notes:

_____

_____

_____

_____

_____

_____

_____

_____

_____

Refer to page 286 in your text for correct answers

Figure 24
The hypothalamus
Fill in the diagram with the appropriate terms.

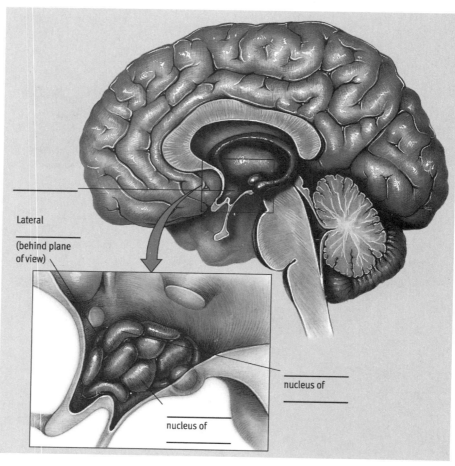

Lateral
_____

(behind plane
of view)

nucleus of
_____

nucleus of
_____

Notes:

_____

_____

_____

_____

_____

_____

_____

_____

_____

Refer to page 379 in your text for correct answers

Figure 25
The amygdala and fear
Fill in the diagram with the appropriate terms.

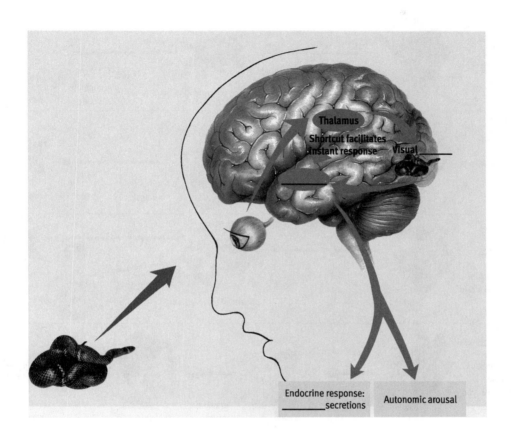

Thalamus

Shortcut facilitates
instant response

Visual

Endocrine response:
_____secretions

Autonomic arousal

Notes:

_____

_____

_____

_____

_____

_____

_____

_____

_____

Refer to page 401 in your text for correct answers

Figure 26
Theories of emotion
Fill in the diagram with the appropriate terms.

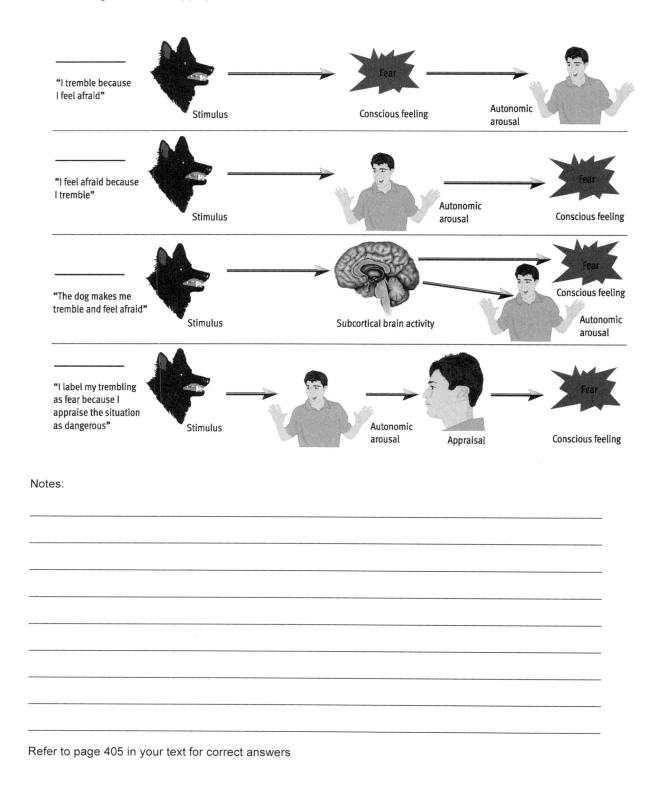

Notes:

_____

_____

_____

_____

_____

_____

_____

_____

_____

Refer to page 405 in your text for correct answers

Figure 27
Erikson's stage theory

Fill in the diagram with the appropriate terms.

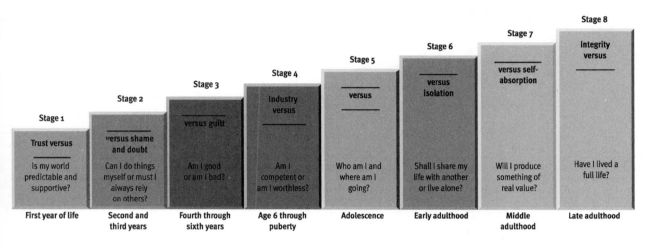

Notes:

_____

_____

_____

_____

_____

_____

_____

_____

Refer to page 431 in your text for correct answers

Figure 28
Piaget's stage theory
Fill in the diagram with the appropriate terms.

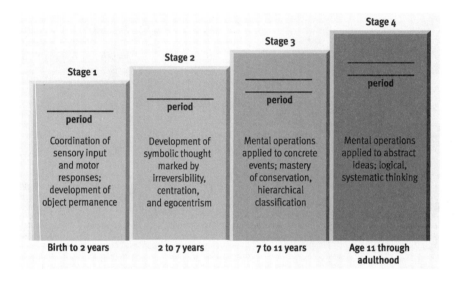

Notes:

_____

_____

_____

_____

_____

_____

_____

_____

_____

Refer to page 433 in your text for correct answers

Figure 29
Kohlberg's stage theory

Fill in the diagram with the appropriate terms.

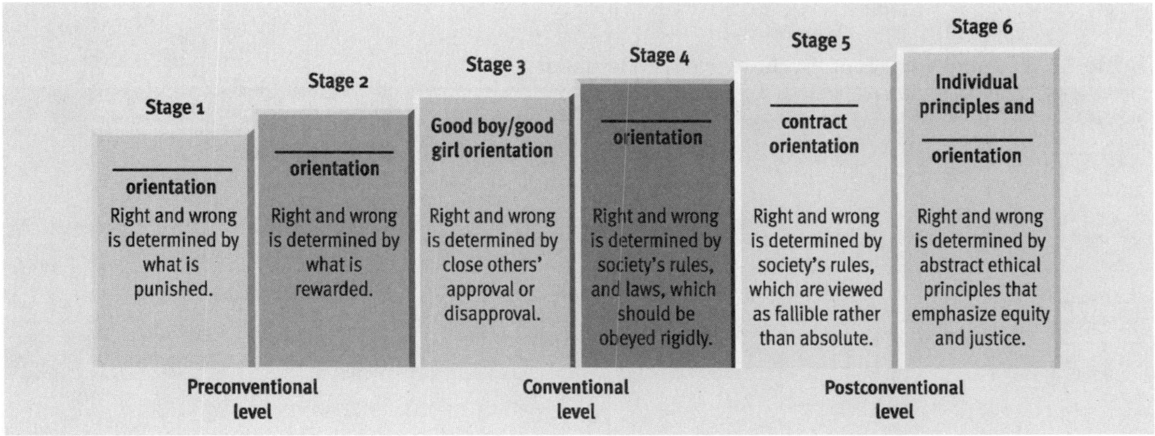

Stage 1	Stage 2	Stage 3	Stage 4	Stage 5	Stage 6
_____ orientation	_____ orientation	Good boy/good girl orientation	_____ orientation	_____ contract orientation	Individual principles and _____ orientation
Right and wrong is determined by what is punished.	Right and wrong is determined by what is rewarded.	Right and wrong is determined by close others' approval or disapproval.	Right and wrong is determined by society's rules, and laws, which should be obeyed rigidly.	Right and wrong is determined by society's rules, which are viewed as fallible rather than absolute.	Right and wrong is determined by abstract ethical principles that emphasize equity and justice.
Preconventional level		Conventional level		Postconventional level	

Notes:

_____

_____

_____

_____

_____

_____

_____

_____

_____

Refer to page 440 in your text for correct answers

Figure 30
Freud's Stages of Psychosexual Development
Fill in the table with the appropriate terms.

Table 12.2   Freud's Stages of Psychosexual Development

Stage	Approximate Ages	Erotic Focus	Key Tasks and Experiences
_____	0–1	Mouth (sucking, biting)	Weaning (from breast or bottle)
_____	2–3	Anus (expelling or retaining feces)	Toilet training
_____	4–5	Genitals (masturbating)	Identifying with adult role models; coping with Oedipal crisis
_____	6–12	None (sexually repressed)	Expanding social contacts
_____	Puberty onward	Genitals (being sexually intimate)	Establishing intimate relationships; contributing to society through working

Notes:

_____

_____

_____

_____

_____

_____

_____

_____

_____

Refer to page 477 in your text for correct answers

Figure 31
Maslow's hierarchy of needs
Fill in the diagram with the appropriate terms.

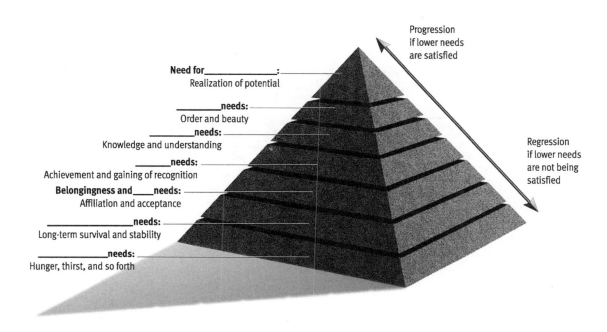

Progression
if lower needs
are satisfied

Need for_____:_____
Realization of potential

_____needs:_____
Order and beauty

_____needs:_____
Knowledge and understanding

_____needs:_____
Achievement and gaining of recognition

Belongingness and____needs:_____
Affiliation and acceptance

_____needs:_____
Long-term survival and stability

_____needs:_____
Hunger, thirst, and so forth

Regression
if lower needs
are not being
satisfied

Notes:

_____

_____

_____

_____

_____

_____

_____

_____

_____

Refer to page 489 in your text for correct answers

Figure 32
Schizophrenia and the ventricles of the brain
Fill in the diagram with the appropriate terms.

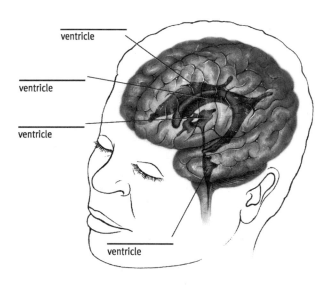

ventricle

ventricle

ventricle

ventricle

Notes:

_____

_____

_____

_____

_____

_____

_____

_____

_____

Refer to page 578 in your text for correct answers

Figure 33
Antidepressant drugs' mechanisms of action
Fill in the diagram with the appropriate terms.

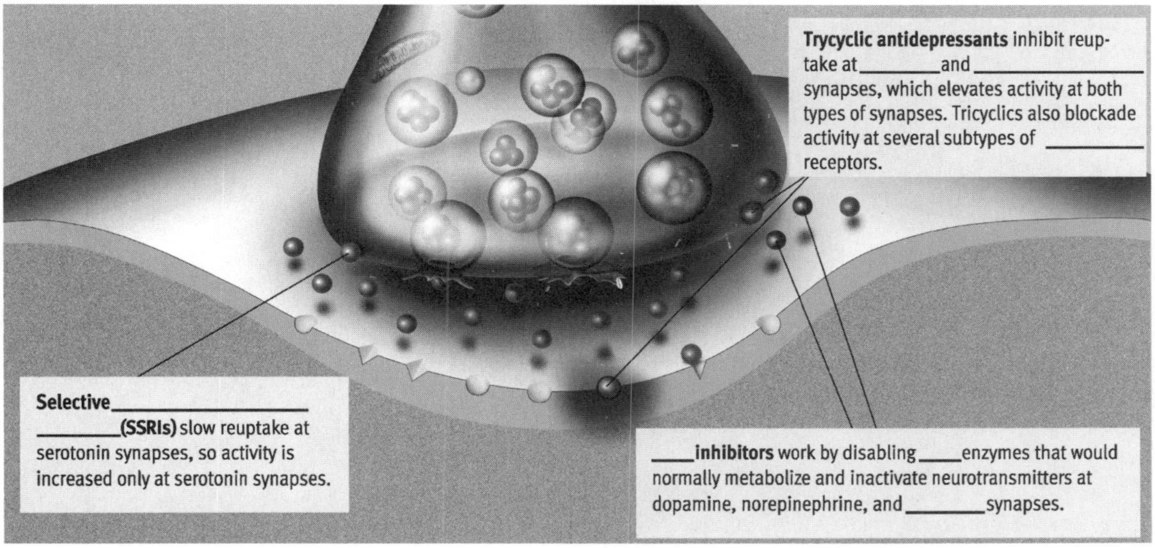

Trycyclic antidepressants inhibit reuptake at_____and_____ synapses, which elevates activity at both types of synapses. Tricyclics also blockade activity at several subtypes of _____ receptors.

Selective_____ _____(SSRIs) slow reuptake at serotonin synapses, so activity is increased only at serotonin synapses.

_____**inhibitors** work by disabling_____enzymes that would normally metabolize and inactivate neurotransmitters at dopamine, norepinephrine, and_____synapses.

Notes:

_____

_____

_____

_____

_____

_____

_____

_____

_____

Refer to page 612 in your text for correct answers